Farm Animals

FIRST EDITION
Series Editor Deborah Lock; **Designer** Sadie Thomas; **US Editor** Elizabeth Hester;
Pre-Production Producer Nadine King; **Producer** Sara Hu;
DTP Designer Almudena Díaz and Pilar Morales; **Jacket Designer** Simon Oon;
Reading Consultant Linda Gambrell, PhD

THIS EDITION
Editorial Management by Oriel Square
Produced for DK by WonderLab Group LLC
Jennifer Emmett, Erica Green, Kate Hale, *Founders*

Editors Grace Hill Smith, Libby Romero, Michaela Weglinski;
Photography Editors Kelley Miller, Annette Kiesow, Nicole DiMella;
Managing Editor Rachel Houghton; **Designers** Project Design Company;
Researcher Michelle Harris; **Copy Editor** Lori Merritt; **Indexer** Connie Binder; **Proofreader** Larry Shea;
Reading Specialist Dr. Jennifer Albro; **Curriculum Specialist** Elaine Larson

Published in the United States by DK Publishing
1745 Broadway, 20th Floor, New York, NY 10019

Copyright © 2023 Dorling Kindersley Limited
DK, a Division of Penguin Random House LLC
23 24 25 26 27   10 9 8 7 6 5 4 3 2 1
001–333429–Apr/2023

All rights reserved.
Without limiting the rights under the copyright reserved above, no part of this publication may be reproduced, stored in or introduced into a retrieval system, or transmitted, in any form, or by any means (electronic, mechanical, photocopying, recording, or otherwise), without the prior written permission of the copyright owner.
Published in Great Britain by Dorling Kindersley Limited

A catalog record for this book
is available from the Library of Congress.
HC ISBN: 978-0-7440-6683-8
PB ISBN: 978-0-7440-6684-5

DK books are available at special discounts when purchased in bulk for sales promotions, premiums, fundraising, or educational use. For details, contact: DK Publishing Special Markets, 1745 Broadway, 20th Floor, New York, NY 10019
SpecialSales@dk.com

Printed and bound in China

The publisher would like to thank the following for their kind permission to reproduce their images:
a=above; c=center; b=below; l=left; r=right; t=top; b/g=background

123RF.com: Olga Itina 24-25; **Agefotostock.com:** imagebroker 14-15; **Dreamstime.com:** Melanie Hobson 12cl; **Shutterstock.com:** Bigandt.com 15t
Cover images: *Front:* **Dreamstime.com:** Kateryna Firsova b; **Shutterstock.com:** Merggy, Pogorelova Olga crb; *Back:* **Dreamstime.com:** Ernest Akayeu cla

All other images © Dorling Kindersley

For the curious
www.dk.com

Farm
Animals

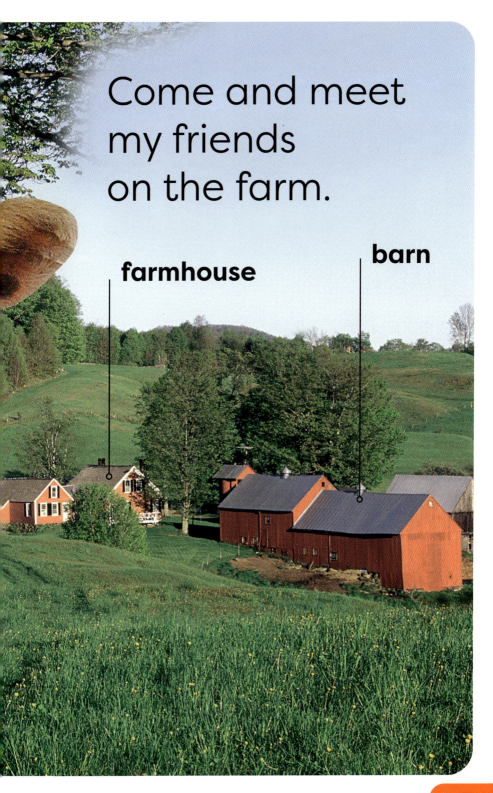

Come and meet my friends on the farm.

farmhouse

barn

Here is the chicken with her little chicks.

chick

Here is the turkey coming to meet you.

snood

 **turkeys**

feathers

Here is the pig.
Here are three
pink piglets.

piglet

pigs

ear

Here are the cows looking at you.

udder

 cows

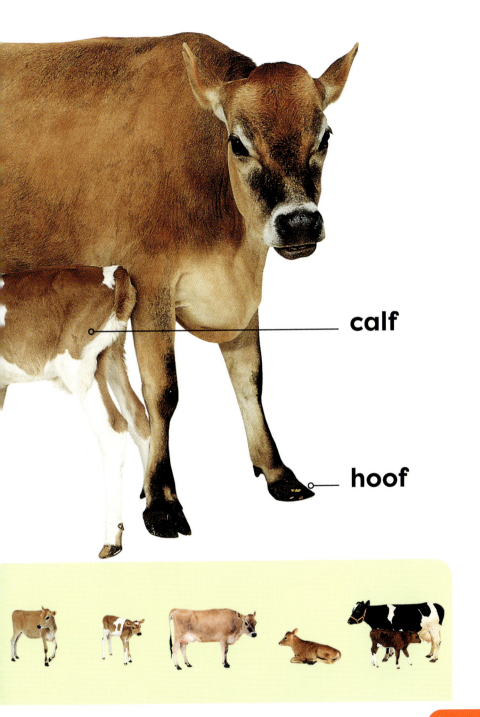

Here is the dog.
Here are her
sleepy puppies.

nose

puppy

dogs

15

Here is the sheep with two little lambs.

lamb

sheep

nose

goats

Here is the goat
lying down
with her kid.

kid

Here are the ducks with their fluffy ducklings.

beak

 **ducks**

duckling

Here are the white geese looking around.

geese

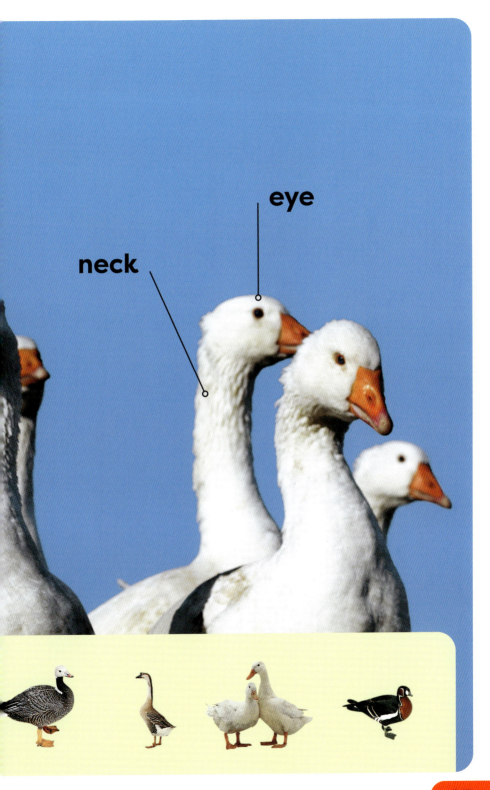

Here is the horse running with her foal.

horses

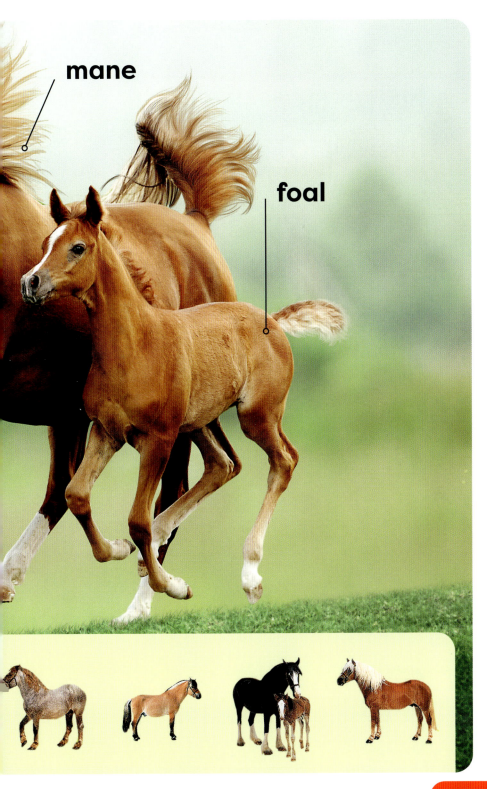

Here are two little ponies.

pony

ponies

Here is the cat curled up with her kitten.

kitten

cats

ear

Come see us again soon!

Glossary

chicken
a bird that is raised by people for its eggs

cow
a large, hoofed animal that is kept for its milk

dog
a four-legged animal that can herd sheep and cows

horse
a hoofed animal used for riding and farm work

sheep
an animal with a thick coat that is raised for wool

Quiz

Answer the questions to see what you have learned. Check your answers with an adult.

Which animal am I?

1. I am a baby chicken.
2. I am a pink animal with a round snout and big ears.
3. I am a baby cow.
4. I am a baby sheep.
5. I am a bird that likes to swim.

1. A chick 2. A pig (or piglet) 3. A calf 4. A lamb 5. A duck